Wildflowers

By Richard Parker

 Publishing, Inc.

105 NE 25th St.   P.O. Box 371005   Miami, Fl. 33137

Contents

Contents

Introduction

The wildflowers identified in this book are all found in Florida, and many are found throughout the eastern half of the United States, even into Canada to the north and the West Indies to the south.

Because of the vast number of wildflowers found in Florida, it is virtually impossible to include all species in one book. What has been attempted here is to present a book of autumn wildflowers which are in bloom during September, October and November. Many wildflowers have a long blooming period and therefore many of the species in this book also bloom during the spring and summer months, or even throughout the year.

The wildflowers in this book are grouped by color. There are five color divisions: White/Cream, Green, Red/Pink, Blue/Violet and Yellow/Orange. Within each color division, wildflowers are grouped alphabetically by family, and then by scientific name.

When attempting to identify wildflowers, do not let color overly effect your decisions: some wildflowers have a wide range of colors, and may vary from the color of the photograph. For example, the moth mullein , *Verbascum blattaria,* may be white or bright yellow. In this book only the white variety is pictured. Wildflowers in the Red/Pink and Blue/Violet divisions are particularly variable in color. Do not hesitate to check the other color groups if the specimen cannot be found in the obvious color section.

It is very important to note the leaf arrangement and leaf shape. Carefully check the leaf information noted for each species. When wildflowers look very much alike, like the sunflowers, leaves are the only clue to indentifying the species. Every effort was made to minimize the use of technical terms in the descriptions, but some are necessary to accurately describe the flower parts that will help to identify a wildflower correctly. These terms are explained in the glossary and botanical diagrams.

Florida has a wide range of habitats which support great numbers of wildflowers during the autumn months. Pinelands are found throughout most of the state, and hammocks, swamps and marshes are interspersed among them.

Coastal dunes often offer a variety of wildflowers. A number of morning-glory species can be found creeping along sandy beaches, and on the Atlantic coast, sea rocket, *Cakile lanceolate,* and firewheel, *Gaillardia pulchella,* nod in the breeze.

Swamp forests are areas usually flooded by shallow waters. Here many wildflowers may be found in bloom throughout the year. Closely related to the swamp forests is the Everglades. The Everglades is a huge, trackless, fresh water marsh that covers most of Florida south of Lake Okeechobee. The Everglades is a wilderness of swamps, hammocks and pools rich with many varieties of wildflowers.

Along the seacoast in the southern portion of the state, mangroves of different species can be found, usually bordered by coastal marshes. In this habitat water varies from saline to brackish, and therefore is dominated by salt-loving plants.

This wide range of habitats provides beautiful and interesting locales for seeking out Florida's fauna, and the wildflowers are as varied as the terrain. However, the best place to look for wildflowers is along the roadsides. Ninety percent of the wildflowers in this book were photographed along the roadsides; the rest, in wildlife parks like Everglades National Park and Corkscrew Swamp Sanctuary.

Glossary

achene a dry, hard, woody-like fruit with one seed, like a sunflower seed

alternate arranged along a stem at different levels not directly opposite each other

anther enlarged head of the stamen which contains the pollen

axil the place where the leaf joins the stem

bract modified leaf that is at the base of the flower head; sometimes mixed with flowers; frequently colored

bearded tufted with hairs

calyx the outer circle or cup of floral leaves which consists of the petal-like sepals; usually green

carpel part of the flower which contains the ovule and, after fertilization, the seed(s)

clasping base of leaf partly surrounds the stem

compound leaf divided into two or more smaller leaflets

corolla collectively, all the petals of the flower

disk in composite family, the round or button-like center which is made up of many flowers having a tubular corolla

dissected leaves that are deeply cut into many segments

floret a small flower; in composite family, one of the disk flowers

inflorescence the arrangement of a group of flowers or flower borne on one main stalk

involucre a circle of bracts supporting a flower head

leaflet a segment of a compound leaf

linear long, narrow leaves with parallel margins

lobed leaf having several indentations in the margin which are less than half way to the base

nerve a rib in a leaf

opposite leaves growing in pairs at the same level on opposite sides of the stem

oval elliptical

ovary part of the pistil which is made up of one or more carpels, inside which the ovules are contained

ovate leaf with broader end at base, tapering upward

ovule the female sex cell within the ovary which develops into the seed after fertilization

palmate compound leaf having multiple leaflets arising from the same place at the top of the leafstalk

panicle inflorescence with alternately arranged and branched flower stalks; each branch has several flowers in a loose cluster

pappus hairs, bristles or scales at the tips of the achenes in the composite family

perianth modified leaves which form outer part of a flower; may be applied to outer whorl of a flower that does not have separate petals and sepals, or to calyx and corolla collectively

petal modified leaf which forms part of the corolla and may be large and/or brightly colored

pinnate compound leaf having many leaflets on both sides of the midrib in a feather-like arrangment

pistil collectively, the female organs of a flower consisting of an ovary at the base, a slender stalk called a style and a divided or knobbed tip called the stigma

pollen tiny grains, each containing a male sex cell, which are produced in the anther

raceme inflorescence with one main axis bearing a number of stalked flowers

ray flower a type of flower in the composite family which has a long, strap-shaped corolla; many of these flowers form the petals of the disk

recurved bent backward or downward

rosette circular cluster of leaves or other flower parts, often at the base of the stem

sepal modified leaf which is one segment of the calyx; usually green

spike inflorescence with stalkless, usually small, flowers densely packed on a single stem

spur hollow, tubular projection from the base of a petal or sepal

stamen male organ of a flower consisting of the pollen bearing anther borne atop a stalk, the filament

standard a single, erect, tree-like stem

stigma flat surface at the top of the style which receives the pollen

style the connecting stalk between the ovary and the stigma

umbel flat-topped inflorescence in which the flower stalks radiate from a common base

whorl circular arrangement of leaves or flower parts around a stem

Floral Structure

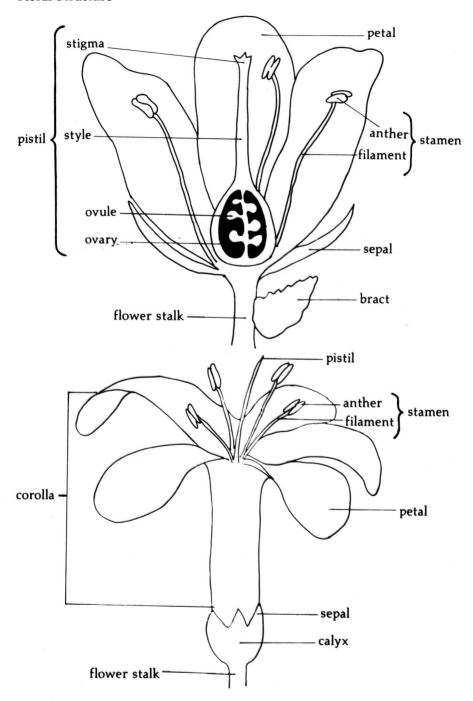

Inflorescence Forms

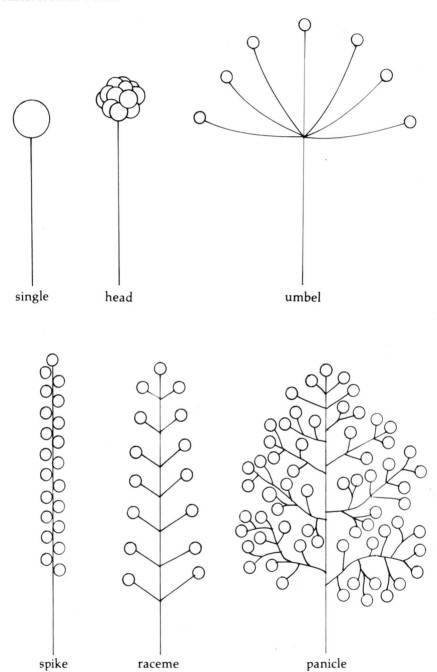

single   head   umbel

spike   raceme   panicle

Leaf Shapes

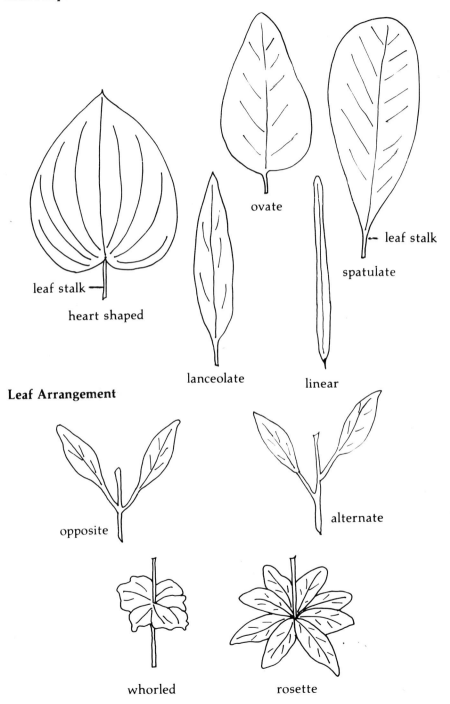

ovate

leaf stalk

spatulate

leaf stalk

heart shaped

lanceolate

linear

Leaf Arrangement

opposite

alternate

whorled

rosette

Leaf Margins

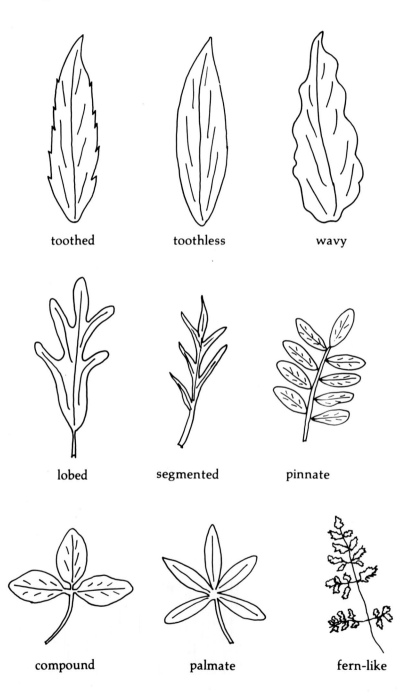

toothed   toothless   wavy

lobed   segmented   pinnate

compound   palmate   fern-like

Arrowhead Family *Alismataceae*

Grass-leaved Arrowhead *Sagittaria graminea*
White three-petaled flower blooming on a long stiff stem in a whorl of threes; three sepals; six stamens. Leaves basal; variable; lanceolate, narrow ribbon-like; toothless; long stalked. Blooms June-September in shallow waters, swamps, marshes, bogs and lakes. Range: Ontario to Minnesota, south to the Gulf States.

Broad-leaved Arrowhead
Sagittaria latifolia
White three-petaled flowers on showy spikes; flowers in whorls of threes. Leaves are **basal**; arrowhead shaped; toothless; long stalked. Blooms July-October in swamps, marshes, bogs, lakes and ponds. Range: Nova Scotia to Ontario and Minnesota, south to Texas and Florida.

White/Cream   13

Amaranth Family *Amaranthaceae*

Cottonweed *Froelichia floridana*

Tiny, flask-shaped whitish woolly flowers in spikes chiefly formed of bracts. Leaves opposite; narrow; toothless; stalkless. Blooms throughout the year in sandy soil and along beaches. Range: Indiana to Minnesota, south to the Gulf States.

Amaryllis Family *Amaryllidaceae*

String Lily
Crinum americanum

Six long, slender white petals that droop and curve back under at the tips; very long stamens; 3-6 inches across. Leaves basal; strap shaped; toothless; 2-4 feet long. Blooms June-October in marshy areas and ditches in the coastal plain. Range: The Gulf States.

White/Cream

Amaryllis Family   *Amaryllidaceae*

Midwestern Spiderlily   *Hymenocallis occidentalis*
Three to six white flowers in a cluster; flowers are long, stalk-like perianth tubes that flare sharply into six long, very narrow petal-like segments. Leaves are basal; strap-like; very long; toothless. Blooms May-June along marshy banks of streams. Range: South Carolina to Missouri, south to the Gulf States.

Milkweed Family   *Asclepiadaceae*

Feay's Milkweed
Asclepias feayi
Small white-petaled flowers in flat clusters; five anther-like hoods are purplish. Leaves opposite; very thin and narrow; toothless; stalkless; 1-4 inches long. Blooms June-October in pinelands. Range: Florida.

White/Cream

Milkweed Family *Asclepiadaceae*

Sarcostemma *Sarcostemma clausum*
White flower having five spreading, blunt petals and a corolla of five roundish, inflated sacs. Leaves opposite; ovate; toothless; stalked. Blooms throughout the year in hammocks, thickets and along lakes. Range: Florida.

Pink Family *Caryophyllaceae*

Bouncing-bet
Saponaria officinalis
Pale pink or whitish five-petaled flowers blooming in a dense cluster; ends of petals notched. Leaves opposite; lanceolate; toothless; 2-3 inches long. Blooms July-September in waste areas along roadsides and railroads. Range: New Brunswick to Ontario and Minnesota, south to the Gulf States.

White/Cream

Composite Family *Compositae*

Common Yarrow *Achillea millefolium*
The dense, flat-topped, terminal clusters of flowers are white, pink or purplish; 4-6 rays; numerous blossoms. Leaves alternate; lancolate; finely dissected into many very slender segments; has a very strong distinctive odor. Blooms September-October in fields, waste areas and along roadsides. Range: New Brunswick to Ontario and Minnesota, south to the Gulf States.

White Old Field Aster *Aster pilosus*
Numerous white flowers which bloom along the upper side of the branches; long stalked; 15-25 rays; sometimes pale purplish rays. Leaves alternate; lanceolate; toothless; stalkless; stiff. Blooms August-November in dry thickets, fields, meadows and along roadsides. Range: Maine to Ontario and Minnesota, south to the Gulf States.

Shepherd's Needle   *Bidens leucantha*
White five-rayed flowers with a yellow center; about 1 inch across; arises from leaf axils on long stalks. Leaves opposite; divided in threes; lanceolate; toothed. Blooms throughout the year in waste areas and sandy soils. Range: Florida.

Pilewort
Erechities hieracifolia
Rayless flowers; cylindrical involucre containing a number of tubular whitish flowers. Leaves alternate; lanceolate; toothed; short stalked; 2-8 inches long. Blooms July-October in moist thickets, open woods, waste areas and burned areas. Range: Quebec to Ontario and Minnesota, south to the Gulf States.

White/Cream

Composite Family *Compositae*

Horseweed
Erigeron canadensis

Tiny whitish-green flowers with very few rays which are compressed and do not spread; numerous flowers. Leaves alternate; linear; toothed; stem bristly. Blooms July-November in fields, waste areas and roadsides. Range: New Brunswick to Ontario and Minnesota, south to the Gulf States.

Boneset *Eupatorium perfoliatum*

10-20 tiny, white, tubular blossoms in flat-topped clusters. Leaves are opposite, joined together at base; lanceolate; toothed; wrinkled; hairy plant. Blooms August-October in thickets, woods and meadows. Range: Quebec to Ontario and Minnesota, south to the Gulf States.

White/Cream   19

Composite Family *Compositae*

Late Flowering Thoroughwort *Eupatorium serotinum*
Numerous small, whitish, fuzzy heads in flat-topped clusters. Leaves opposite; arrowhead shaped; toothed; long stalked; three veined. Blooms June-September in thickets, fields and along the edges of woods. Range: New Jersey to Minnesota, south to the Gulf States.

False Boneset
Kuhnia eupatorioides
Ten to 25 tubular, creamy-white to purplish flowers in loose terminal clusters. Leaves alternate; lanceolate; toothed; stalks are short; 1-4 inches long; mostly a hairy plant. Blooms June-October in woods, thickets, fields and meadows. Range: New Jersey and Pennsylvania to Illinois and Missouri, south to the Gulf States.

White/Cream

Composite Family *Compositae*

Toothed White-topped Aster *Seriocarpus asteroides*
White rayed flowers in flat-topped clusters; 4-5 rays. Leaves alternate; spatulate; narrow-based; toothed in middle. Blooms June-October in dry woods. Range: Maine to Michigan, south to Alabama, Mississippi and Florida.

Seriocarpus *Seriocarpus bifoliatus*
White flower with about five rays which are broad and short; bracts whitish with green tips; disk flowers cream; flat-topped clusters. Leaves alternate; oval-ovate; toothless; stalkless; numerous. Blooms June-September in pinelands on the coastal plain. Range: Virginia to Louisiana and Florida.

White/Cream

Composite Family *Compositae*

White Crownbeard *Verbesina virginica*
Dense, flat-topped crown of white flowers; 3-5 rays; has a frosty appearance. Leaves alternate; lanceolate to largely ovate; toothed; stalked. Blooms July-October in woods, thickets, waste areas and along streams. Range: Ohio to Illinois and Iowa, south to the Gulf States.

Morning-glory Family *Convolvulaceae*

Moonflower *Calonyction aculeatum*
Large white bell-shaped flower. Leaves alternate; heart shaped; toothless; indented base; stalked. Blooms June-September in wet areas, along roadsides and beaches. Range: Florida.

White/Cream

Morning-glory Family   *Convolvulaceae*

Field Bindweed   *Convolvulus arvensis*
Small white or pink bell-shaped flowers an inch or less across; no bracts at base; a vine. Leaves alternate; triangular shaped; blunt tips; toothless; short stalked. Blooms May-September in fields, meadows, waste areas and along roadsides. Range: Nova Scotia to Quebec and Ontario, south to the Gulf States.

Hedge Bindweed   *Convolvulus sepium*
White or pink trumpet-shaped blossoms on long stalks arising from leaf axils; 2-3 inches across; large heart-shaped bracts at base of flower. Leaves alternate; triangular or arrowhead shaped; basal lobes short and blunt; toothless; stalked; 2-5 inches long. Blooms May-September in fields, thickets, waste areas, meadows and roadsides. Range: Quebec to Ontario, south to the Gulf States.

White/Cream   23

Morning-glory Family   *Convolvulacea*

Common Dodder
Cuscuta gronovii

Blossoms are waxy-white, five-petaled, bell-shaped corollas; a parasitic vine. Leaves reduced to scales. Blooms August-October in fields, meadows, waste areas, and along streams. Range: Quebec to Ontario, south to the Gulf States.

Wild Potato-vine   *Ipomoea pandurata*

Blossoms are large, white, bell-shaped flowers; five sepals united at the base; purple blotch in center; up to 3 inches across; a vine. Leaves alternate; heart shaped; toothless; stalkless; midrib, stalks and margins often purplish. Blooms June-September in fields, waste areas, meadows and roadsides. Range: Connecticut and New York to Ontario, south to the Gulf States.

White/Cream

Morning-glory Family   *Convolvulaceae*

White Seaside Morning-glory   *Ipomoea stolonifera*
Large white bell-shaped flowers with bright yellow centers. Leaves alternate; variable; cleft into 3-5 round-ended lobes, or leaves can be oblong and unlobed; long stalked. Blooms June-October on coastal sand dunes. Range: South Carolina, south to the Gulf States.

Cucumber Family   *Cucurbitaceae*

One-seeded Bur-cucumber
Sicyos angulatus
Clusters of whitish-cream five-petaled blossoms; stamen bearing flowers at tips of long stalks; pistil bearing flowers on shorter stalks; clustered fruits are covered with prickles. Leaves alternate; lobed; toothed margins; maple-like. Blooms July-October in woods, thickets and by rivers, streams. Range: Maine and Quebec to Ontario and Minnesota, south to the Gulf States.

White/Cream

Sedge Family *Cyperaceae*

Star Rush *Dichromena colorata*
Small unattractive flowers arranged in scaly-bracted, cone-shaped clusters. Leaves alternate on stem; long; slender; grass-like; long leaf-like bracts surrounding flowers are mostly white with green tips. Blooms March-November in moist and wet areas. Range: North Carolina to Georgia, south to the Gulf States.

Pipewort Family *Eriocaulaceae*

Ten-angled Pipewort
Eriocaulon decangulare
Whitish, woolly flower heads at the ends of long, stiff stems. Leaves basal; long; slender; grass-like; toothless. Blooms June-November in wet areas, roadside ditches and the coastal plain. Range: North Carolina to Georgia, south to the Gulf States.

White/Cream

Spurge Family   *Euphorbiaceae*

Spurge Nettle   *Cnidoscolus stimulosus*
A corolla-like calyx with five petal-like lobes is the stamen bearing flower; the pistil is greenish and not showy. Leaves alternate; heart shaped; deeply lobed; toothed; long stalked; 2-10 inches long; covered with bristle-like stinging hairs. Blooms March-September in sandy pinelands, waste areas, fields and roadsides. Range: Virginia, south to the Gulf States.

September Croton   *Croton glandulosus septentrionalis*
Tiny unattractive whitish flowers arising out of leaf axils. Leaves opposite; lanceolate to oblong; toothed; hairy stem. Blooms July-October in fields, pastures, waste areas and roadsides. Range: Delaware to Illinois and Missouri, south to the Gulf States.

White/Cream   27

Spurge Family *Euphorbiaceae*

Flowering Spurge *Euphorbia corollata*
The five round, whitish petals are really sepals surrounding the very tiny flower cluster; numerous in a flat-topped cluster. Leaves alternate; oval; toothless; stalkless; bright green. Note whorl of small leaves at base of branching flower stalks. Blooms June-October in fields, meadows, open woods, waste areas and roadsides. Range: New York to Ontario and Minnesota, south to the Gulf States.

Gentian Family *Gentianaceae*

Elliott's Sabatia *Sabatia brevifolia*
White to cream colored five-petaled flowers in a terminal cluster. Leaves opposite; linear; toothless; stalkless; stem slightly ridged. Blooms September-October in coastal plain pinelands. Range: South Carolina, south to Alabama and Florida.

28   White/Cream

Mint Family *Labiatae*

Musky Mint *Hyptis alata*
White flowers in oval-shaped heads clustered on a tall plant. Leaves opposite; lanceolate; toothed; woolly underneath. Blooms throughout the year in moist pinelands, swamps and hammocks. Range: North Carolina, south to the Gulf States and the West Indies.

Pea Family *Leguminosae*

Hog Peanut *Amphicarpa bracteata*
Blossoms are whitish or purplish pea-like flowers in drooping clusters; arises from leaf axils; vine-like. Leaves alternate; stalked; three leaflets; ovate; toothless. Blooms July-September in woods and thickets. Range: Quebec to Ontario and Minnesota, south to the Gulf States.

White/Cream   29

Pea Family   *Leguminosae*

Hairy Bush-clover   *Lespedeza hirta*
Blossoms whitish or yellowish-white with a purplish base; tight flower heads with stalks longer than leaf stalks. Leaves alternate; short stalked; three leaflets; ovate; toothless. Blooms July-October in woods, thickets and fields. Range: Maine to Ontario, south to the Gulf States.

White Sweet Clover   *Melilotus alba*
Blossoms are numerous white flowers arranged in long, narrow clusters arising from leaf axils; plants have a vanilla-like odor when crushed or dried. Leaves alternate; stalked; three leaflets; toothed; each leaflet notched at tip. Blooms May-October in fields, meadows and roadsides. Range: New Brunswick to Ontario and Minnesota, south to the Gulf States and the West Indies.

White/Cream

Pea Family   *Leguminosae*

White Clover   *Trifolium repens*

Blossoms are white or pinkish, globe-shaped heads; long stalked; separate from leaves. Leaves alternate; long stalked; three leaflets, toothed; tip of each leaflet notched. Blooms April-October in fields, meadows, waste areas, and along roadsides. Range: New Brunswick to Ontario and Minnesota, south to the Gulf States.

Lily Family   *Liliaceae*

Yucca   *Yucca flaccida*

Numerous bell-shaped waxy-whitish flowers on a central woody stalk. Leaves basal; rosette; long and slender; grass-like blades; rigid; sharp tips. Blooms June-September in sandy soil, dunes, pine barrens and the coastal plain. Range: North Carolina to Tennessee, south to the Gulf States.

White/Cream

Mallow Family *Malvaceae*

Swamp Rose Mallow
Hibiscus moscheutos
Five showy rose-like petals that are white or pinkish with a red or purple center; long style tipped with five round stigmas; up to 8 inches across. Leaves alternate; heart shaped; may be three pointed; toothed; long stalked. Blooms June-September in bogs, marshes and other wet areas. Range: Kentucky to Indiana, Illinois and Missouri, south to the Gulf States.

Meadow-beauty Family *Melastomataceae*

Maryland Meadow-beauty
Rhexia mariana
Whitish or pale pink flowers have four lopsided petals and curved yellow stamens. Leaves opposite; lanceolate; toothed. Blooms May-October in meadows, thickets, woods, wet sands, pine barrens and roadsides. Range: Massachusetts to Kentucky, south to the Gulf States.

White/Cream

Waterlily Family *Nymphaeaceae*

Fragrant Waterlily *Nymphaea odorata*
White (sometimes pinkish) fragrant flowers with petals broadest at the center. Leaves roundish with a V-shaped notch at the base; both flowers and leaves float on water. Blooms June-September in ponds, lakes and fast moving streams. Range: New Brunswick to Ontario and Minnesota, south to the Gulf States.

Orchid Family *Orchidaceae*

Nodding Lady's Tresses *Spiranthes cernua*
Small white flowers arranged in a double spiral. Leaves basal; grass-like; toothless. Blooms September-November in bogs and meadows. Range: Nova Scotia to Ontario and Minnesota, south to the Gulf States.

White/Cream

Pokeweed Family *Phytolaccaceae*

Pokeweed
Phytolacca americana

Whitish-green flowers in long narrow clusters; 5 sepals; no petals; flowers opposite leaves; fruit purplish-black. Leaves alternate; lanceolate; toothless; margins may be wavy; 5-10 in. long. Blooms June-October in woods, thickets, fields and waste areas. Range: Maine to Ontario and Minnesota, south to the Gulf States.

Plantain Family *Plantaginaceae*

English Plantain   *Plantago lanceolata*

Short, bushy flower heads tightly packed with numerous small white flowers on long, grooved stalks. Leaves basal; long tapering; toothless; three-ribbed. Blooms April-November in waste areas, yards, parks and along roadsides. Range: New Brunswick to Ontario and Minnesota, south to the Gulf States.

White/Cream

Milkwort Family *Polygalaceae*

Whorled Milkwort *Polygala verticillata*
Dense cone-shaped clusters of small whitish or greenish flower heads at the tips of long slender stalks. Leaves whorled; very narrow leaves; toothless; stalkless; 3-7 inches long. Blooms June-September in fields, open woods and waste areas. Range: Maine to Ontario, south to Virginia, Tennessee and Louisiana.

Buckwheat Family *Polygonaceae*

Dog Tongue *Eriogonum tomentosum*
Whitish flower is six sepals and nine stamens mixed with leaf-like bracts. Leaves whorled in threes, fours or fives; ovate; toothless; stalkless. Blooms July-September in dry pinelands and sandhills on coastal plains. Range: South Carolina to Alabama and Florida.

White/Cream   35

Buckwheat Family   *Polygonaceae*

Jointweed
Polygonella polygama

Tiny pink or white flowers, each having five sepals and eight stamens; numerous in showy spikes. Leaves alternate; very narrow; toothless; stalkless. Blooms June-September in sandhills and pinelands. Range: Georgia to Missouri, south to the Gulf States.

Coastal Smartweed
Polygonum setaceum

Small whitish or pinkish flowers in spikes; achenes are three-angled. Leaves alternate; lanceolate; sharp, pointed tips; toothless; short stalked; stem reddish; long bristles on the sheaths at the nodes. Blooms August-October on coastal plains. Range: Massachusetts to Arkansas, south to the Gulf States.

White/Cream

Buckwheat Family *Polygonaceae*

Virginia Knotweed
Tovara virginiana

Tiny whitish flowers scattered along a long, slender stalk; seeds jump off stalk when touched. Leaves alternate; ovate; toothless; 2-6 inches long. Blooms July-October in woods and thickets. Range: New Hampshire to Quebec and Ontario, south to the Gulf States.

Wintergreen Family *Pyrolaceae*

Indian Pipe *Monotropa uniflora*
Entire plant is waxy-white with a single flower drooping downward from the end of a scaly stem; contains no chlorophyll; has a ghostly appearance; 4-5 petals; no stamens; plant turns blackish with age. Leaves absent. Blooms June-October in woods. Range: New Brunswick to Ontario and Minnesota, south to the Gulf States.

White/Cream 37

Bedstraw Family *Rubiaceae*

Buttonbush
Cephalanthus occidentalis

Flowers are in dense ball-shaped heads covered with long, protruding stamens, somewhat resembling a pincushion. Leaves opposite; oval; toothless; short stalked; 8 inches long. Blooms June-October in swamps, marshes, bogs, along rivers, streams and ponds. Range: Nova Scotia to Quebec and Ontario, south to the Gulf States.

Buttonweed *Diodia virginiana*
Small whitish-bluish four-petaled flowers in leaf axils; two long stamens. Leaves opposite; lanceolate; toothless; stalkless. Blooms June-September in swamps, ponds, streams, wet fields and ditches. Range: New Jersey to Illinois and Missouri, south to the Gulf States.

White/Cream

Bedstraw Family *Rubiaceae*

Richaria *Richaria scabra*
Tiny whitish-pinkish six-petaled flowers in dense clusters. Leaves opposite; lanceolate to ovate; toothless; stalkless. Blooms July-September in wet areas, swamps, ponds and lakes. Range: Virginia to Arkansas, south to the Gulf States.

Lizard-tail Family *Sauraceae*

Lizard's Tail *Saururus cernuus*
Flowers are in long, slender tapering and drooping clusters; blossoms are small, fragrant white flowers. Leaves alternate; heart shaped; 3-6 inches long; toothless. Blooms May-September in swamps and shallow water. Range: Rhode Island to Quebec and Ontario, south to the Gulf States.

White/Cream

Snapdragon Family *Scrophulariaceae*

Clammy Hedge Hyssop *Gratiola neglecta*
Tiny whitish-pinkish five-petaled flowers on long stalks out of main leaf axils. Leaves opposite; lanceolate; toothed; stalkless. Blooms May-October in swamps, marshes, lakes, ponds and canal ditches. Range: Maine to Quebec and Ontario, south to Florida.

Moth Mullein
Verbascum blattaria
Blossoms are yellow-white five-petaled flowers widely spaced along the upper stem; stamens bearded with violet hairs. Leaves alternate; ovate-lanceolate; toothed; stalkless to clasping. Blooms June-September in fields, meadows, waste areas and along roadsides. Range: Maine and Quebec to Ontario, south to the Gulf States.

White/Cream

Snapdragon Family *Scrophulariaceae*

Culver's Root
Veronicastrum virginicum

Blossoms are tiny whitish tube-like flowers in slender, tapering, dense spikes; two projecting stamens. Blooms June-September in meadows, thickets, woods and along roadsides. Range: Vermont to Ontario, south to the Gulf States.

Tomato Family *Solanaceae*

Jimsonweed
Datura stramonium

Blossoms are large white, lavender or violet trumpet-like flowers; five-pointed lobes on corolla rim; 3-4 inches long; fruit pods spiny. Leaves alternate; ovate; oak-like; irregularly toothed; 3-8 inches long. Blooms July-September in fields, waste areas and along roadsides. Range: Nova Scotia to Quebec and Ontario, south to the Gulf States.

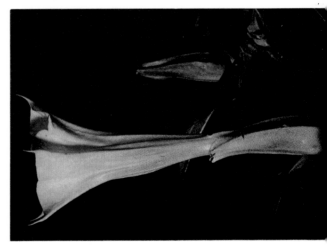

White/Cream   41

Parsley Family *Umbelliferae*

Queen Anne's Lace
Daucus carota

Blossoms are umbels of tiny white flowers in a flat-topped cluster having a lacy appearance; sometimes a single, deep purple floret is found in the center. Leaves alternate, pinnately divided and deeply cut into numerous narrow segments. Blooms May-October in fields, meadows, waste areas and roadsides. Range: New Brunswick to Ontario and Minnesota, south to the Gulf States.

Many-flowered Water Pennywort   *Hydrocotyle umbellata*
Very tiny white flowers in umbels on long stalks arising from a creeping stem. Leaves alternate; roundish; lobed margins; very long stalked. Blooms June-September in swamps, marshes, bogs, shores and wet ditches. Range: North Carolina, south to the Gulf States.

White/Cream

Parsley Family *Umbelliferae*

Water Parsnip *Sium suave*
Tiny white flowers in umbels of 2-4 inches across; tall, erect branching stem that is longitudinally furrowed. Leaves alternate, pinnately divided; five or more lanceolate, toothed leaflets. Blooms June-September in swamps, meadows and muddy places. Range: Ontario to Minnesota, south to Missouri and Florida.

Verbena Family *Verbenaceae*

White Vervain
Verbena urticifolia
Blossoms are very tiny white flowers arranged in several long and slender spikes; not as showy as other vervains. Leaves opposite; lanceolate; toothed. Blooms June-September in woods and thickets. Range: Maine to Quebec and Ontario, south to the Gulf States.

Amaranth Family *Amaranthaceae*

Slender Green Amaranth *Amaranthus hybridus*

Greenish flowers mixed with long, bristle-like bracts in long, slender, nodding spikes. Leaves alternate; oval; toothless; pointed tips; well stalked. Blooms August-October in waste areas and along roadsides. Range: Quebec to Ontario, south to Iowa and the Gulf States.

Green Amaranth
Amaranthus retroflexus

Greenish flowers mixed with long bristle-like bracts in dense spikes. Leaves alternate; oval; toothless; pointed tips; well stalked. Blooms August-October in fields, waste areas and along roadsides. Range: New Brunswick to Ontario and Minnesota, south to the Gulf States.

Cashew Family *Anacardiaceae*

Winged Sumac
Rhus copallina
Small yellowish-green flowers in dense clusters. Leaves alternate; divided into 9-21 leaflets; ovate-lanceolate; toothed; stems are winged. Blooms May-November in thickets, open woods, along railroads and roadsides. Range: Maine to Michigan, south to Missouri and the Gulf States.

Milkweed Family *Asclepidaceae*

Milkweed *Asclepias tomentosa*
Large pale yellowish-green petaled flowers having hood-like cups with curved horns projecting from the top. Leaves opposite; oval; toothless; very short stalked; softly downy. Blooms May-October in sandy pine barrens. Range: North Carolina, south to the Gulf States.

Green

Milkweed Family *Asclepidaceae*

Whorled Milkweed *Asclepias verticillata*
Blossoms have five greenish-white corolla lobes; white anther-like hoods; five sepals barely attached to base; pod fruits contain seeds with silky hairs. Leaves whorled; narrow; toothless; stalkless; 3-7 in whorl; margins rolled. Blooms June-Sept. in woods and fields. Range: New York to Ontario, south to the Gulf States.

Cynanchum
Cynanchum scoparium

Tiny yellowish-green flowers with pointed corolla lobes; small scattered clusters of blossoms on a vine. Leaves alternate; very narrow; toothless; short stalked; up to 2 inches long. Blooms April-October in hammocks on the coastal plain. Range: South Carolina to Florida.

Green

Pea Family *Leguminosae*

Bahama Lysiloma
Lysiloma bahamensis

Small, greenish-white, globe-shaped flowers on long stalks. Leaves alternate; pinnately divided into 2-6 pairs of pinnate segments which are again divided into numerous oblong leaflets; toothless. Blooms August-October around water. Range: Florida.

Saxifrage Family *Saxifragaceae*

Ditch Stonecrop *Penthroum sedoides*

Blossoms lack petals but have five small, yellowish-green sepals and ten stamens. Leaves alternate; lanceolate; toothed; 2-4 inches long. Blooms July-October in wet areas, swamps, and along stream banks and ditches. Range: Maine to Quebec to Ontario and Minnesota, south to the Gulf States.

Green

Acanthus Family *Acanthaceae*

Dicliptera *Dicliptera assurgens*
Bright red or crimson, two-lipped flowers with only two stamens; corolla is curved; in spikes mixed with leaf-like bracts. Leaves alternate; ovate-lanceolate; toothless. Blooms throughout the year in the southern hammock portion of the state. Range: Florida.

Milkweed Family *Asclepiadaceae*

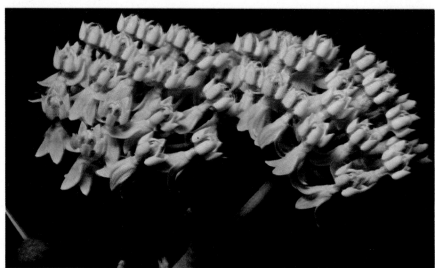

Swamp Milkweed *Asclepias incarnata*
Pink flowers with five reflexed petals with anther-like hoods. Leaves alternate; lanceolate; toothless; short stalked. Blooms May-September in swamps, marshes, bogs and other wet areas. Range: Maine to Quebec and Ontario, south to the Gulf States.

Pink/Red

Bignonia Family *Bignoniaceae*

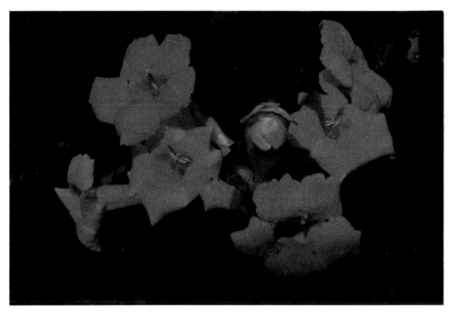

Trumpet Creeper *Campsis radicans*
Bright orange or reddish-orange trumpet-like flowers up to 3 inches long; showy clusters. Leaves opposite; 7-11 ovate leaflets; sharply toothed; a vine that climbs by aerial rootlets on stem. Blooms June-September in woods, thickets, fence rows, walls and yards. Range: Connecticut to Michigan and Iowa, south to the Gulf States.

Honeysuckle Family *Caprifoliaceae*

Trumpet Honeysuckle
Lonicera sempervirens
Bright red trumpet-shaped flowers with yellow within the throat; in whorled clusters; a woody vine. Leaves opposite; upper joined around stem; ovate; toothless; stalked. Blooms April-September in woods, thickets and fence rows. Range: Maine to Iowa, south to Gulf States.

Spiderwort Family   *Commelinaceae*

Aneilema   *Aneilema nudiflorum*
Tiny white three-petaled flowers strongly tipped with rose-purple; arises from leaf axils. Leaves alternate; lanceolate; toothless; clasping; smooth plant. Blooms September-October in swamps, bogs, and along lakes, streams and ponds. Range: Georgia to Florida and the West Indies.

Composite Family   *Compositae*

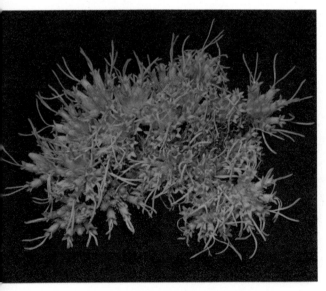

Carphephorus
Carphephorus corymbosus
Rose-colored tubular flowers surrounded by broad, over-lapping bracts; pappus is hair-like bristles; a tall plant, 1-3 feet high. Leaves alternate; spatulate; toothless; pale green; clasping; hairy. Blooms July-September in pinelands and along the coastal plain. Range: North Carolina to Georgia and Florida.

Composite Family *Compositae*

Field Thistle *Cirsium discolor*
Purple blossoms containing a large number of slender tubular flowers compacted tightly together; the feathery pappus develops into seed-like fruits which have a silky parachute-like attachment. Leaves alternate; lanceolate; deeply lobed with erect, sharp spines; no spines on stem. Blooms July-October in woods, fields and along roadsides. Range: Maine to Quebec and Ontario, south to Missouri and Florida.

Smooth Elephant's Foot *Elephantopus nudatus*
Tubular purple flowers surrounded by large leaf-like bracts in clusters at the ends of branches. Leaves rosette; ovate-oval; toothed; 2-10 inches long; few leaves on stem. Blooms July-September in open woods, sandy soils, and along roadsides. Range: Delaware to Arkansas, south to Florida.

Pink/Red

Composite Family *Compositae*

Devil's Grandmother
Elephantopus tomentosus
Pink tubular flowers in clusters surrounded by leaf-like bracts. Leaves basal rosette; ovate-oval; toothed; very few leaves along stem. Blooms July-September in dry woods. Range: Maryland to Kentucky, south to the Gulf States.

Hollow Joe-pye-weed *Eupatorium fistulosum*
Purple, lilac or pink flowers massed in rounded or dome-like clusters; each flower head contains 5-8 tubular florets. Leaves whorled; lanceolate; toothed; 4-12 inches long; stem green-purplish tinged; hollow. Blooms July-September in moist meadows and thickets. Range: Maine to Quebec, west to Iowa, south to the Gulf States.

Pink/Red

Composite Family   *Compositae*

Sweet Joe-pye-weed   *Eupatorium purpureum*
Fuzzy, full, pale pinkish-purple flowers in a dome-shaped cluster. Leaves whorled; 3 or 4 leaves in whorls; ovate-lanceolate; toothed; stalked; odor of vanilla when crushed. Blooms July-September in woods, thickets, and along roadsides. Range: New Hampshire to Minnesota, south to Arkansas and Florida.

Firewheel
Gaillardia pulchella
The large crimson or purplish rayed flowers are often tipped with yellow; bracts of flower heads taper into narrow points; fringe of large hairs near base; tip of petals three-clefted. Leaves alternate; sharply toothed; lanceolate. Blooms May-September in dry areas and along the eastern coastline. Range: Maine to Minnesota, south to the Gulf States.

Pink/Red

Composite Family *Compositae*

Dense Gayfeather
Liatris spicata

Rose-purple tubular flowers in long, narrow clusters; each head contains 5-15 florets. Leaves alternate; linear; toothless; stalkless; 5-15 inches long. Blooms July-October in wet open woods, fields, and along roadsides. Range: Maine to Ontario and Wisconsin, south to Missouri, Louisiana and Florida.

Grass-leaf Barbara's-buttons *Marshallia graminifolia*
Pink, flaring, five-lobed flowers having slender tubes; bluish anthers; numerous flowers crowded on a roundish center. Leaves alternate; grass-like; toothless; stalkless. Blooms July-September in moist coastal plain pinelands and savannahs. Range: North Carolina, south to Louisiana and Florida.

Pink/Red

Composite Family   *Compositae*

Climbing Hempweed   *Mikania scandens*
Whitish to pale purplish tubular flowers in heads clustered at the tips of long stalks
arising from leaf axils; only composite that is a vine. Leaves opposite; arrowhead
shaped; toothed; stalked; 2-4 inches long. Blooms July-October in swamps, bogs,
thickets. along stream banks and roadsides. Range: Maine to Ontario, south to
Missouri and Florida.

Vanilla Plant   *Trilisa odoratissima*
Rose-purple flowers are small, numerous and tubular; in flat-topped terminal
clusters. Leaves alternate on stem; small; basal, lanceolate shaped; broader through
the middle; toothless; 4-10 inches long; vanilla-like odor when crushed. Blooms
August-October in dry and wet coastal plain pinelands. Range: North Carolina,
south to Louisiana and Florida.

Pink/Red   55

Composite Family   *Compositae*

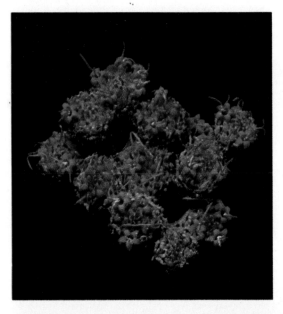

Hairy Trilisa
Trilisa paniculata
Rose-purple tubular flowers arranged in a narrow cluster on the upper part of the stem. Leaves alternate on stem; narrow; small; basal lanceolate shaped; broader through the middle; hairy. Blooms August-October in meadows, fields, pinelands, and along roadsides. Range: North Carolina, south to Louisiana and Florida.

Baldwin's Ironweed   *Vernonia baldwini*
Purplish flowers in dense, flat-topped clusters; flower bracts are green with purple edges; bract tips curve outward and downward. Leaves alternate; lanceolate-ovate; toothed; woolly underneath. Blooms July-October in fields, meadows, and along roadsides. Range: Illinois, Missouri and Arkansas, south to the Gulf States.

Morning-glory Family   *Convolvulaceae*

Small Red Morning-glory   *Ipomoea coccinea*
Small scarlet, bell-shaped flowers; a vine. Leaves alternate; heart shaped; toothless; long stalked. Blooms July-October in waste areas and along streams. Range: New York to Michigan and Missouri, south to the Gulf States.

Railroad-vine   *Ipomoea pes-caprae*
Large purplish, bell-shaped flowers. Leaves alternate; roundish; toothless; folds along the mid-vein; thick; bright green; stalked. Blooms June-October on coastal sand dunes. Range: Georgia and the Gulf States.

Morning-glory Family *Convolvulaceae*

Scarlet Morning-glory   *Ipomoea quamoclit*

Scarlet bell-shaped flowers with a long corolla; long stalked. Leaves alternate; ovate; sharp gradual point; heart-shaped base; toothless; long stalked. Blooms July-October in fields and waste areas. Range: Virginia to Missouri, south to the Gulf States.

Arrow-leaf Morning-glory   *Ipomoea sagittata*

Rosy pink bell-like flowers with long stalks; up to 3 inches across. Leaves alternate; arrowhead shaped; two basal lobes pointing outward; toothless; long stalked. Blooms July-September in swamps, marshes and coastal sand dunes. Range: North Carolina, south to the Gulf States.

Pink/Red

Mustard Family *Cruciferae*

Sea Rocket   *Cakile lanceolata*
Small pinkish four-petaled flowers in dense clusters. Leaves alternate; lanceolate; toothless; fleshy. Blooms June–October in sandy soil. Range: Florida.

Spurge Family *Euphorbiaceae*

Fire-on-the-mountain   *Euphorbia heterophylla*
Unattractive greenish flowers consisting of a stamen or stalked pistil having three united carpels in a cup-like involucre. Leaves on stem alternate; leaves surrounding the cup-shaped involucres are whorled; stalked; bright red blotches at base of whorled leaves. Blooms June–September in thickets, waste areas, open woods and moist sandy soil. Range: Virginia to Minnesota, south to the Gulf States.

Pink/Red

Gentain Family *Gentianaceae*

Slender Marsh Pink
Sabatia campanulata

Pink five-petaled flower with a yellow center; sepals project beyond petals. Leaves opposite; linear; toothless. Blooms July–September in sandy places on coastal plains. Range: Massachusetts, south to Louisiana and Florida.

Mint Family *Labiatae*

False Dragonhead *Physostegia virginiana*
Pale purple or rose hooded flower with a spotted three-lobed lip; tubed corolla. Leaves opposite; lanceolate; toothed; short stalked; stem is square. Blooms June-September in meadows, bogs and along streams. Range: Quebec to Minnesota, south to the Gulf States.

Pink/Red

Pea Family   *Leguminosae*

Naked Tick-trefoil   *Desmodium nudiflorum*

Pink pea-like flowers on a tall, slender leaf-less stalk arising out of a whorl of leaves that are divided into three leaflets. Leaves are ovate; toothless; long stalked. Lower portion of plant is brushy and leafy. Blooms July-September in woods. The flat, oval-shaped fruit, called "sticktights", is better known. Range: Maine to Quebec and Minnesota, south to Gulf States.

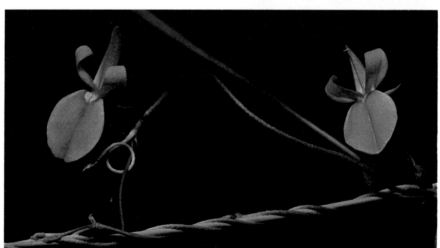

Milk Pea   *Galactia regularis*

Violet-purple flower with lower petal long and curved. Leaves alternate; stalked; divided into three leaflets; ovate; toothless. Blooms June-September in woods, thickets, along railroads and roadsides. Range: Missouri to Tennessee, south to Georgia, Florida and the West Indies.

Pink/Red

Pea Family *Leguminosae*

Sensitive Plant *Mimosa strigillosa*
Tiny, deep pink flowers crowded in oblong heads; arise from leaf axils on long stalks; rough, hairy fruit pods. Leaves alternate; pinnately divided into several pairs of long segments that are again divided pinnately into smaller leaflets. Blooms April-November in pinelands, hammocks, meadows and along banks of streams. Range: the Gulf States.

Red Clover *Trifolium pratense*
Blossoms are purplish-pink and are in dense, roundish cone-shaped heads having a pair of leaves at the base. Leaves alternate; divided into threes; well stalked; toothed; a V-shaped pattern on each leaflet. Blooms April-October in fields, meadows, waste areas, and along roadsides. Range: New Brunswick to Ontario, south to the Gulf States.

Pink/Red

Lily Family   *Liliaceae*

Southern Red Lily   *Lilium catesbaei*
Each stem bears a single scarlet, six-petaled flower densely spotted with purple; long and slender stalks; base of petals yellow; long pointed tips curve outward. Leaves alternate; lanceolate; toothless; stalkless. Blooms July-September in wet pinelands and savannahs of the coastal plain. Range: Virginia to Florida and Louisiana.

Lobelia Family   *Lobeliaceae*

Cardinal Flower
Lobelia cardinalis
Bright scarlet, tubed flower with two upper petals and three lower; stamen projects upward through the cleft in the corolla. Leaves alternate; lanceolate; toothed; stalked; 2-6 inches long. Blooms July-October in wet meadows, thickets, swamps, bogs and along streams. Range: New Brunswick to Ontario, south to the Gulf States.

Pink/Red

Mallow Family   *Malvaceae*

Halberd-leaf Rose Mallow   *Hibiscus militaris*
Hollyhock-like pink flower has five showy rose-like petals and a purple center; long style tipped with five round stigmas; up to 8 inches across. Leaves alternate; lanceolate; three-pointed; center point very long; two side points much shorter; toothed; stalked. Blooms July-September in marshes, swamps, bogs and wet areas. Range: Pennsylvania to Minnesota, south to the Gulf States.

Fern Rose
Kosteletzkya virginica
The pink, five-petaled flowers arise from leaf axils. Leaves alternate; ovate; toothed; indented base; rough down of hairs. Blooms throughout the year in marshes, swamps, bogs and wet ditches. Range: New York, south to the Gulf States.

Pink/Red

Mallow Family *Malvaceae*

Turk's Cap
Malvaniscus grandiflorus
Bright drooping scarlet flower that never completely opens; long, protruding stamens. Leaves alternate; lanceolate; toothed; short stalked. Blooms throughout the year in waste areas and yards. Range: Gulf States to the West Indies.

Meadow-beauty Family *Melastomataceae*

Nash's Meadow-beauty
Rhexia nashii
Four-petaled rose-purple flowers with long, slender, curving yellow stamens. The leaves are opposite; lanceolate; toothless; stalkless; taper to a point. Blooms May-October in fields, clearings, along moist ditches. Range: Virginia and Tennessee, south to Louisiana and Florida.

Pink/Red

Meadow-beauty Family *Melastomataceae*

Nuttall's Meadow-beauty
Rhexia nuttallii
Pink four-petaled flower with a yellow stamen in center. Leaves opposite; ovate; prickly margins; stalkless. Blooms March-September in sandy soils. Range: Florida and Georgia.

Wood-sorrel Family *Oxalidaceae*

Violet Wood-sorrel *Oxalis violacea*
Blossoms are rose-purple or violet five-petaled flowers on separate stalks than leaves. Leaves basal; long stalked; divided into threes; tips notched; toothless; shorter stalks than flower stalks. Blooms August-October in woods, thickets, meadows and fields. Range: Vermont to Minnesota, south to the Gulf States.

Pink/Red

Buckwheat Family *Polygonaceae*

Pennsylvania Smartweed *Polygonum pensylvanicum*
Tight clusters of pinkish flowers are actually colored sepals; 4-6 stamens; a pistil with two or three styles. Leaves alternate; lanceolate; toothless; 2-10 inches long. Blooms July-October in woods, thickets and waste areas. Range: Ontario to Minnesota, south to the Gulf States.

Purslane Family *Portulacaceae*

Purslane *Portulaca pilosa*
Pink to rose-purple five-petaled flowers growing low to the ground; yellow stamen in center. Leaves opposite or alternate; linear; toothless; succulent. Blooms May-October in sandy woods, along beaches and roadsides. Range: Gulf States.

Pink/Red   67

Wintergreen Family   *Pyrolaceae*

Pinesap   *Monotropa hypopithys*
Tiny reddish and yellowish flowers, hang with open ends down; as the fruit matures, the stem straightens and the open ends point upwards. Leaves absent; thick, fleshy stem has scales. Blooms June-October in woods. Range: Quebec to Ontario and Minnesota, south to the Gulf States.

Pitcher-plant Family   *Sarraceniaceae*

Fiddler's Trumpet
Sarracenia leucophylla
Large, reddish flower having five petals, five sepals, three bracts; pistil's style is shaped like an umbrella. Leaves are distinct and may be more easily identifiable than the blossoms. Leaves are erect; flaring trumpets with a stiff, standing, ruffled hood; strong red veins. Blooms April-July with the leaves lasting into October in swamps, marshes, bogs on coastal plain. Range: Florida to Georgia and Mississippi.

Pink/Red

Snapdragon Family *Scrophulariaceae*

False Foxglove
Agalinis fasciculata

Pink-purple flower has five spreading lobes, and a dark spotted throat with some yellow; has a long stalk; numerous. Leaves opposite; linear; toothless; stalkless. Blooms July-October in fields, meadows, sand dunes, and along marsh edges and roadsides. Maryland to Tennessee, south to Louisiana and Florida.

Large Purple Gerardia
Gerardia purpurea

Pink-purple tubular bell-like flowers in leaf axils; dark spots within the throat. Leaves opposite; linear; toothless; stalkless; sometimes smaller leaves in axils. Blooms August-October in fields, thickets and bogs. Range: Massachusetts to Minnesota, south to the Gulf States and the West Indies.

Vervain Family *Verbenaceae*

Fog Fruit *Lippia lanceolata*

Tiny white, pink or bluish five-petaled flowers crowded on a small, scaly-bracted head on a long stalk arising from leaf axil. Leaves opposite; lanceolate; toothed; 1-3 inches long; trailing stem. Blooms May-September in wet areas, waste areas, and along banks of streams. Range: Ontario to Minnesota, south to the Gulf States.

Rose Verbena *Verbena canadensis*

Violet, lavender, purple or rose flower with five flaring lobes; dense clusters. Leaves opposite; maple-like toothed; blunt tips; lobed or cleft; stalkless. Blooms April-October in sandy soil, rocky areas and along roadsides. Range: Pennsylvania to Minnesota, south to the Gulf States.

Pink/Red

Vervain Family *Verbenaceae*

Tampa Vervain *Verbena tampensis*
Tiny rose colored five-petaled flowers in dense clusters at tips of long stems. Leaves opposite; ovate-lanceolate; sharply toothed. Blooms May-October in sandy soil of hammocks and open woods. Range: Florida.

Moss Verbena *Verbena tenuisecta*
Showy rose-purple, pink or white five-petaled flowers in flat-topped clusters. Leaves opposite; very finely disected; sprawling, hairy plant. Blooms June-September in coastal plains and along roadsides. Range: South Carolina to Missouri, south to the Gulf States.

Pink/Red   71

Acanthus Family   *Acanthaceae*

Smooth Ruellia   *Ruellia strepens*
Lavender-blue showy trumpet-like flowers in leaf axils; long stalked. Leaves opposite; ovate-lanceolate; toothless; stalked; two small leaves at base of flower. Blooms July-September in woods, thickets and fields. Range: New Jersey and Pennsylvania to Illinois and Iowa, south to Texas and Florida.

Forget-me-not Family   *Boraginaceae*

Viper's Bugloss   *Echium vulgare*
Dark blue flowers blooming in a showy spike; long red stamens project; two stamens are crossed; upper lip longer than lower lip; one flower blooms at a time; a bristly plant. Leaves alternate; oblong-lanceolate; toothless; short stalked; hairy; 1-6 inches long. Blooms June-September in waste areas, near streams and along roadsides. Range: Quebec to Ontario and Minnesota, south to the Gulf States.

Spiderwort Family   *Commelinaceae*

Common Dayflower
Commelina communis
Blossoms are two large blue petals with a lower, smaller white petal; three sepals; often roots at joint of stems. Leaves alternate; lanceolate-ovate; toothless. Blooms July-October in woods, thickets and around ponds and lakes. Range: Massachusetts to Wisconsin, south to the Gulf States.

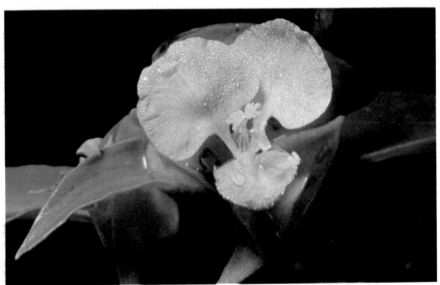

Virginia Dayflower   *Commelina virginica*
Blossoms are two large blue upper petals with a smaller blue lower petal; three green sepals; leaf sheaths are fringed with reddish hairs. Leaves alternate; lanceolate; toothless. Blooms July-October in moist woods, thickets and around ponds and small lakes. Range: New Jersey and Pennsylvania to Missouri, south to the Gulf States.

Blue/Violet

Composite Family   *Compositae*

Bushy Aster   *Aster dumosus*
15-25 pale lavender-bluish rayed flowers on long slender branchlets. Leaves alternate; narrow; toothless; stalkless; leaves on flower branchlets are crowded and bractlike. Blooms August-October in sandy fields and thickets. Range: New York to Ontario, south to the Gulf States.

Late Purple Aster   *Aster patens*
Deep blue-violet rayed flowers at ends of slender branchlets; 15-25 rays; bracts sticky, rough and tips spreading. Leaves alternate; ovate-oblong; toothless; stalkless; leaf base lobed; stem hairy. Blooms August-October in open woods and fields. Range: Maine to Minnesota, south to Missouri and Florida.

Composite Family   *Compositae*

Mistflower   *Eupatorium coelestinum*
Bright violet-blue tubular flowers in bell-shaped heads arranged in dense flat-topped clusters. Leaves opposite; arrowhead shaped; margins mostly rounded; lobe-like; stalked; 1-3 inches long. Blooms July-October in woods, thickets and along stream banks. Range: New Jersey and Pennsylvania to Illinois and Missouri, south to the Gulf States and the West Indies.

Blue Lettuce   *Lactuca floridana*
Small blue aster-like flowers in loose panicles. Leaves alternate; lanceolate; usually deeply lobed; toothed. Blooms July-October in fields and at the edges of woods. Range: Massachusetts to Minnesota, south to the Gulf States.

Morning-glory Family   *Convolvulaceae*

Ivy-leaved Morning-glory   *Ipomoea hederacea*
Blue, pink or white bell-shaped flowers on long stalks. Leaves alternate; three-lobed; toothed; long stalked. Blooms June-October in fields, meadows and waste areas. Range: New York to Ontario and Minnesota, south to the Gulf States.

Jacquemontia   *Jacquemontia tamnifolia*
Small blue funnel-shaped flowers in a dense cluster mixed with hairy bracts. Leaves alternate; ovate; toothless; sometimes indented at base. Blooms August-September in fields and thickets on the coastal plain. Range: Virginia to Arkansas, south to Mississippi and Florida.

Blue/Violet

Gentian Family   *Gentianaceae*

Seaside Gentian   *Eustoma exaltatum*
Purple or blue flower having a flaring corolla with five lobe-like petals; yellow stamens; flowers at tips of stems. Leaves opposite; ovate-oval; toothless; stalkless. Blooms all year in pinelands, hammocks and coastal sands. Range: Florida.

Waterleaf Family   *Hydrophyllaceae*

Skyflower   *Hydrolea corymobsum*
Five-petaled azure blue flowers in flat-topped clusters at top of plant; long stamens. Leaves alternate; lanceolate; toothless. Blooms July-September in swamps, marshes, bogs and at the edges of woods. Range: South Carolina to Florida.

Blue/Violet

Mint Family   *Labiatae*

Self-heal
Prunella vulgaris

Bluish, lavender or whitish hooded flowers in oblong heads; lower lip fringed; bracts crowded among flowers. Leaves opposite; ovate-lanceolate; toothless to slightly toothed; stem square. Blooms May-October in fields, waste areas, lawns and along roadsides. Range: Quebec to Ontario, south to the Gulf States.

Blue Sage   *Salvia azurea*

Bright blue two-lipped flower with lower lip longer; 12-20 blossoms in an interrupted spike. Leaves opposite; very narrow; toothed or toothless; stalkless. Blooms July-December in fields, pinelands, prairies, along roadsides, and at the edge of woods. Range: Minnesota and Iowa, south to Texas and Florida.

Mint Family *Labiatae*

Downy Skullcap
Scutellaria incana incana
Bluish lipped, hooded flowers in a crowded raceme. Leaves opposite; ovate; toothed; stalked. Blooms June-September in dry woods, clearings, and along roadsides. Range: New Jersey and New York to Illinois, south to Arkansas and Florida.

Blue Curls *Trichostema dichotomum*
Violet-blue, hooded flowers on long stalks in leaf axils; long curved stamens separate this mint from all others. Leaves opposite; ovate; toothless; short stalked; smaller leaves in lower leaf axils. Blooms August-October in dry woods, fields and along roadsides. Range: Maine to Michigan, south to Missouri and the Gulf States.

Blue/Violet

Pea Family   *Leguminosae*

Spurred Butterfly-pea   *Centrosema virginianum*

Violet colored flower with a large, broad standard up to an inch across; there is a spur-like projection near the base on the backside. Leaves alternate; divided into three leaflets; toothless; lanceolate; stalked; 1-2 inches long. Blooms June-September in open woods and fields. Range: New Jersey to Arkansas, south to the Gulf States.

Butterfly-pea
Clitoria mariana

Blossoms are pale lavender-blue or violet; the large, rounded petal is notched at the tip; the keel and wing petals are very short. Leaves alternate; three leaflets; ovate; toothless; stalked. Blooms June-September in woods, thickets and pinelands. Range: New York to Illinois, south to the Gulf States.

Blue/Violet

Pea Family   *Leguminosae*

Kudzu Vine   *Pueraria lobata*
Reddish-purple flowers in a dense cluster. Leaves alternate; divided into three leaflets; ovate; strongly wavy margins; long stalked. Blooms August-September in waste areas, thickets and roadsides. Range: Pennsylvania to Illinois and Missouri, south to Louisiana and Florida.

Lobelia Family   *Lobelioideae*

Glades Lobelia
Lobelia glandulosa
Lavender or blue flower with five petals, two upper, three lower; white eye; flowers usually on one side of stem. Leaves alternate; lanceolate; toothless; stalkless. Blooms throughout the year in bogs, glades, wet pinelands, and the coastal plain. Range: Virginia to Florida.

Blue/Violet

Passion-flower Family *Passifloraceae*

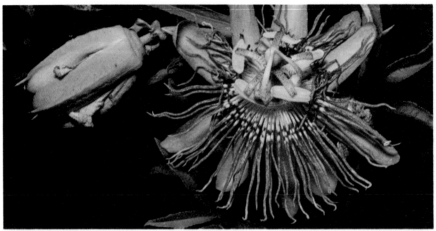

Maypop *Passiflora incarnata*
Lavender colored flower having a striking outer fringed crown that is an inch long and is purple and pink; edible fruit is ovate and yellowish when ripe. Leaves alternate; three-lobed; toothed; stalked. Blooms May-September in woods, thickets, fields and along roadsides. Range: Pennsylvania to Illinois and Missouri, south to the Gulf States.

Pickerelweed Family *Pontederiaceae*

Water Hyacinth *Eichhornia crassipes*
Showy spikes of lavender flowers with upper lobes marked with yellow. Leaves basal; roundish; toothless; floats on water. Blooms throughout the year in ditches, ponds, lakes and streams. Range: Virginia to Missouri, south to the Gulf States and the West Indies.

Blue/Violet

Pickerelweed Family *Pontederiaceae*

Pickerelweed
Pontederia cordata

Bright lavender-blue flowers in a showy spike; middle upper lobe of corolla has two yellow spots. Leaves basal; ovate-lanceolate; toothless; heart-shaped base; long stalked. Blooms May-October in bogs, swamps, marshes, shallow waters and muddy shores. Range: Nova Scotia to Ontario and Minnesota, south to Missouri and Florida.

Snapdragon Family *Scrophulariaceae*

Blue Toadflax
Linaria canadensis

Blue, two-lipped flower with a white palate; short spur. Leaves alternate; linear; toothless; trailing offshoots at base of plant. Blooms April-September in fields, meadows, and at the edges of woods. Range: Nova Scotia to Quebec and Ontario, south to the Gulf States.

Blue/Violet

Snapdragon Family *Scrophulariaceae*

Sharp-winged Monkeyflower *Mimulus alatus*
Blossoms are violet, pink or white two-lipped flowers; three lobes above, two below; short stalked. Leaves opposite; ovate-lanceolate; toothed; stalked; stem with thin wings along angles. Blooms June-September in wet meadows, swamps, bogs, along streams and lakes. Range: Connecticut to Ontario, south to the Gulf States.

Parsley Family *Umbelliferae*

Blue Rattlesnake-masters
Eryngium aquaticum
Round heads of tiny, bluish, five-parted florets, often concealed by bracts. Leaves alternate; lanceolate; variable; strongly toothed; jagged cut edges; prickly-tipped teeth at intervals. Blooms July-September in marshes, bogs, ditches on coastal plains, and along ponds and streams. Range: New Jersey, south to the Gulf States.

Blue/Violet

Vervain Family   *Verbenaceae*

False Vervain
Stachytarpheta jamaicensis

Blue flowers blooming along a long stout stem arising out of leaf axils. Leaves opposite; ovate-lanceolate; toothed; stalked. Blooms throughout the year in pinelands and dunes. Range: Alabama, Florida and the West Indies.

Blue Vervain
Verbena hastata

Tiny, violet-blue, five-petaled flowers arranged in several long and slender spikes; an erect, four-sided hairy stem branching at the top. Leaves opposite; lanceolate; toothed; hairy; 1-5 inches long. Blooms June-September in fields, meadows, and along streams and roadsides. Range: New Brunswick to Ontario and Minnesota, south to the Gulf States.

Blue/Violet

Amaryllis Family *Amaryllidaceae*

Yellow Star-grass *Hypoxis hirsuta*
Bright yellow six-petaled flowers at the top of a hairy stem. Leaves are basal; long; slender; toothless; grass-like; usually longer than flower stalk. Blooms March-September in woods and meadows. Range: Maine to Missouri, south to the Gulf States.

Milkweed Family *Asclepidaceae*

Butterflyweed *Asclepias tuberosa*
Orange-yellow to orange-red flower having five reflexed corolla lobes; central crown of five anther-like hoods, five sepals barely attached to the base; pod fruits contain seeds with silky hairs. Leaves alternate; lanceolate; toothless; short stalks; stem is hairy. Blooms May-September in fields, meadows and along roadsides. Range: Ontario to Minnesota, south to the Gulf States.

Yellow/Orange

Touch-me-not Family *Balsaminaceae*

Spotted Touch-me-not *Impatiens capensis*
Orange flowers more or less spotted with red; long tail-like spur; arises from leaf axils, usually in pairs. Leaves alternate; ovate; toothed; stalked. Blooms June-September in woods, swamps and wet places. Range: Quebec to Ontario and Minnesota, south to the Gulf States.

Composite Family *Compositae*

Wingstem *Actinomeris alternifolia*
Numerous flowers with 2-10 drooping bright yellow rays varying in size; mop-like disk; 1-2 inches across. Leaves alternate; lanceolate; toothed; stalk flows into stem; tips sharply pointed; 4-12 inches long. Blooms June-October in thickets, fields, and along woods and roadsides. Range: Ontario to New York and Missouri, south to the Gulf States.

Composite Family *Compositae*

Coastal Endorima
Balduina angustifolia

Yellow rayed flowers that are three-lobed at the tips; outer bracts are broader than the inner; disk is honeycomb-like. Leaves alternate; very narrow; toothless; numerous. Blooms throughout the year on sandhills and pinelands on the coastal plain. Range: Mississippi to Georgia and Florida.

One-headed Endorima
Baludina uniflora

Single bright yellow flower on a single stout downy stem; 20-30 rays lobed at the tips; large yellowish disk has a honeycomb-like surface. Leaves alternate on stem; narrow; toothless; stalkless; basal leaves broader at tips. Blooms July-September in pinelands, marshes and on the coastal plain. Range: North Carolina to Louisiana and Florida.

Composite Family *Compositae*

Spanish Needles *Bidens bipinnata*
Small, yellow, rayless flowers that turn into clusters of seeds; each seed tipped with four short barbs; clings to clothing. Leaves opposite; much dissected; fern-like; long stalked. Blooms August-October in waste areas and along roadsides. Range: New York to Iowa, south to the Gulf States.

Showy Bur-marigold *Bidens laevis*
Bright yellow rayed flower with 8-10 large petals; dark disk; 1-2 inches across. Leaves opposite; lanceolate; toothed; stalkless; 3-8 inches long. Blooms September-November in swamps, wet meadows, and along streams. Range: New Hampshire to Missouri, south to the Gulf States.

Composite Family   *Compositae*

Hairy Golden Aster   *Chrysopsus subulata*
Yellow rayed aster-like flowers in clusters at tips of long stems. Leaves alternate; lanceolate-narrow; toothless; stalkless; stem and leaves have webby hairs. Blooms May-September in pinelands and scrub. Range: Florida.

Star Tickseed   *Coreopsis pubescens*
Bright yellow flower with 8-10 rays; tips of petals lobed; yellowish disk; involucre's outer bracts are star-like. Leaves opposite; 3-5 segments; lanceolate; toothless; short stalked or stalkless. Blooms July-October in open woods and at edges of woods. Range: Virginia to Illinois and Missouri, south to the Gulf States.

Yellow/Orange

Composite Family *Compositae*

Smooth Hawksbeard *Crepis capillaris*
Small yellow dandelion-like flowers in a branching top. Leaves alternate; lanceolate; lobed or deeply cut; stalkless. Blooms July-October in fields, waste areas, and along roadsides. Range: New York to Missouri, south to the Gulf States.

Bandana Daisy
Gaillardia lanceolata
Yellow rayed flower with a purplish disk; bracts ovate-triangular. Leaves alternate; narrow; toothless. Blooms April-October in pinelands, dry woods and rocky areas. Range: South Carolina to Missouri, and south to the Gulf States.

Composite Family *Compositae*

Haplopappus
Haplopappus divaricatus

Yellow rayed flower with a yellow disk; pappus of unequal lengths; bracts fringed with hairs. Leaves alternate; narrow; toothed; stalkless. Blooms July-October in sandy soil, dry fields, waste areas and open woods. Range: Virginia to Missouri, south to the Gulf States.

Autumn Sneezeweed *Helenium autumnale*

Flower is 10-18 drooping, bright yellow rays; tips of petals are three-lobed; yellowish disk is ball shaped; numerous flowers. Leaves alternate; lanceolate; toothed; stalkless; 2-5 inches long. Blooms September-October in swamps, wet meadows, thickets, and along roadsides. Range: Quebec to Minnesota, south to the Gulf States.

Yellow/Orange

Composite Family *Compositae*

Purple-headed Sneezeweed
Helenium nudiflorium

Bright yellow rayed flower with three-lobed tips on petals; rounded, deep purplish disk; 10-15 rays; numerous flowers. Leaves alternate; lanceolate; not strongly toothed; stalks flow into the stem. Blooms June-October in thickets, meadows, at edge of woods, and along roadsides. Range: Maine to Michigan, south to the Gulf States.

Narrow-leaved Sunflower
Helianthus angustifolius

12-20 bright yellow rays with a dark purplish-brown disk; 2-3 inches across. Leaves alternate; very long and narrow; toothless; stiff and rough; stalkless; 2-7 inches long. Blooms July-October in wet pinelands, swamps, thickets, and wet areas along roadsides. Range: New York to Missouri, south to the Gulf States.

Yellow/Orange

Composite Family *Compositae*

Common Sunflower
Helianthus annuus

Large, golden rayed flower which is the familiar sunflower of North America; large brownish disk; up to 10 inches across. Leaves alternate; heart shaped; toothed; rough; slender stalks; stem hairy. Blooms July-October in fields, meadows, waste areas, and along roadsides. Range: Minnesota to Missouri, south to the Gulf States.

Weak Sunflower
Helianthus debilis

Bright yellow rayed flowers blooming on a semi-reclining, mottled stem. Leaves alternate; lanceolate; toothed; stem rough and hairy. Blooms June-October in waste areas and along roadsides. Range: South Carolina to the Gulf States.

Yellow/Orange

Composite Family *Compositae*

Varied-leaf Sunflower
Helianthus heterophyllus

Bright yellow rayed flower with a dark, purplish-brown disk; about 20 rays. Leaves opposite; upper, very narrow; toothless; stalkless; lower leaves ovate-lanceolate; toothless; long stalked; up to 8 inches long. Blooms August-September in wet coastal plain pinelands, swamps, wet thickets and meadows. Range: North Carolina to Louisiana and Florida.

Coastal Golden Aster
Heterotheca scabrella

Numerous bright yellow rayed flowers in clusters at the ends of long, hairy stems. Leaves alternate; narrow; numerous; toothless; basal leaves spatula shaped; Blooms August-January in coastal plains. Range: Alabama to Florida.

Composite Family   *Compositae*

Hairy Hawkweed
Hieracium gronovii
Yellow dandelion-like flowers having a long stalk; numerous blossoms. Leaves alternate; ovate; stalkless; hairy. Blooms July-October in woods, thickets, and along roadsides: Range: Ontario to Missouri and New York, south to the Gulf States.

Rattlesnake-weed   *Hieracium vernosum*
Small yellow dandelion-like flowers blooming on a very branching plant. Leaves basal; ovate-oval; toothless; red or purple veins stand out plainly. Blooms May-October in open woods. Range: Maine to Michigan, south to Louisiana and Florida.

96

Composite Family *Compositae*

Wild Lettuce
Lactuca canadensis

Many tiny, pale yellow dandelion-like flowers in long, slender clusters; flower head has 10-20 florets. Leaves alternate; lanceolate; toothed; deeply lobed; extremely variable. Blooms July-September in thickets, fields, waste areas, and along roadsides. Range: Quebec to Ontario, south to Missouri and the Gulf States.

Phoebanthus *Phoebanthus grandiflora*

A single-stem plant, usually with one, bright yellow rayed flower facing directly upwards; 16-20 rays; yellowish disk is nearly an inch wide. Leaves alternate; linear; toothless; stalkless; single nerve. Blooms June-September in sandy pinelands and oak scrub. Range: Florida.

Yellow/Orange

Composite Family *Compositae*

Large-flowered Leafcup *Polymnia uvedalia*
Sunflower-like flower with 10-15 bright yellow rays; 1-3 inches across; involucre is cup shaped with large, hairy fringed outer bracts. Leaves opposite; broadly ovate; coarsely angular toothed; maple-like in appearance; stalkless. Blooms July-October in woods, thickets, and along streams. Range: New York to Missouri, south to the Gulf States.

False Dandelion
Pyrrhopappus carolinianus
Pale yellow dandelion-like flowers on long stems. Leaves alternate; upper lanceolate; clasping; lower pinnately lobed, cleft or toothed; 3-8 inches long. Blooms April-September in fields, meadows, and along roadsides. Range: Delaware to Missouri, south to the Gulf States.

Yellow/Orange

Composite Family *Compositae*

Black-eyed Susan
Rudbeckia hirta

10-20 bright orange-yellow rays with an ovate, dark purplish-brown disk; 2-4 inches across. Leaves alternate; lanceolate; toothed; lower leaves long stalked; a hairy plant. Blooms May-October in fields, meadows, waste areas, and along streams and roadsides. Range: British Columbia south to the Gulf States.

Green-headed Coneflower   *Rudbeckia laciniata*
Bright yellow rayed flowers that often have reflexed petals; greenish button-shaped disk. Leaves alternate; deeply cut into 3-5 parts; toothed; stalked. Blooms July-September in thickets, fields, meadows and at the edges of woods. Range: Quebec to Minnesota, south to the Gulf States.

Yellow/Orange

Composite Family   *Compositae*

Late Goldenrod   *Solidago gigantea*
Tiny bright yellow flowers crowded on spreading or recurved branches in a terminal arrangement. Leaves alternate; lanceolate; toothed; stalkless; 3-6 inches long. Blooms July-October in woods, thickets and along roadsides. Range: Quebec to Minnesota, south to the Gulf States.

Grass-leaved Goldenrod   *Solidago graminifolia*
Bright yellow flowers massed in flat-topped clusters. Leaves alternate; lanceolate; toothless; stalkless; rough; 3-7 parallel nerves. Blooms July-October in thickets, wet fields and along roadsides. Range: Quebec and Ontario to Minnesota, south to Texas and northern Florida.

Yellow/Orange

Composite Family *Compositae*

Early Goldenrod *Solidago juncea*
Bright yellow flowers in clusters on spreading branches; 7-12 rays; plume-like appearance. Leaves alternate; upper lanceolate; toothless; smaller wing-like leaflets in leaf axils; lower leaves larger, ovate, toothed. Blooms July-September in fields, meadows, open woods and along roadsides. Range: New Brunswick to Ontario and Minnesota, south to Missouri, Georgia and northern Florida.

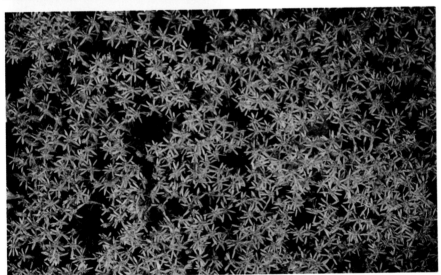

Small-headed Goldenrod *Solidago microcephala*
Tiny bright yellow flowers crowded on spreading or recurved branches. Leaves alternate; linear; toothless. Blooms July-September in sandy soil. Range: New Jersey, south to Mississippi and Florida.

Yellow/Orange

Composite Family *Compositae*

Downy Goldenrod *Solidago puberula*
Golden yellow flowers crowded in a narrow cluster at the tip of the plant. Leaves alternate; narrow; sharply toothed; numerous; 2-4 inches long; stem often purplish. Blooms September-November in sandy or rocky woods, fields and along roadsides. Range: Quebec to Ontario, south to Mississippi and Florida.

Common Dandelion
Taraxacum officinale
Bright yellow flower heads; reflexed outer bracts; fluffy globe-shaped white seedballs. Leaves rosette; narrow-lanceolate; pinnately lobed and jagged; stem hollow and milky. Blooms most of the year in fields, meadows, waste areas and along roadsides. Range: New Brunswick to Ontario and Minnesota, south to the Gulf States.

Yellow/Orange

Composite Family *Compositae*

Wedelia *Wedelia trilobata*
Bright, broad yellow rayed flowers; three lobed or tipped at ends of petals. Leaves opposite; ovate-wedge shaped; sharply toothed; short stalked. Blooms throughout the year around shores of lakes, ponds, swamps and marshes. Range: Florida.

Mustard Family *Cruciferae*

Wild Radish *Raphanus raphanistrum*
Yellow four-petaled flowers with lilac colored veins. Leaves alternate; upper lanceolate, toothed; lower broad and deeply lobed. Blooms April-November in waste areas and along roadsides. Range: Ontario to Minnesota, south to the Gulf States.

St. Johnswort Family *Guttiferae*

Common St. Johnswort *Hypericum perforatum*
Bright yellow five-petaled flowers with bushy stamens; black dots on petal margins; terminal clusters. Leaves opposite; ovate-oblong; toothless; stalkless. Blooms June-September in fields, meadows, waste areas and along roadsides. Range: Quebec to Ontario and Minnesota, south to the Gulf States.

St. Peter's-wort *Hypericum stans*
Bright yellow four-petaled flower with a pair of large sepals and a pair of smaller ones; pistil has three or four styles. Leaves opposite; oval-oblong; toothless; heart-shaped base clasps the stem. Blooms June-October in fields, meadows and dry, sandy, open woods. Range: New York to Missouri, south to the Gulf States.

Yellow/Orange

Pea Family *Leguminosae*

Partridge Pea *Cassia fasciculata*
Bright yellow, five-petaled flower that often has reddish-purple spots at base; ten stamens—four have yellow anthers and six have purple ones. Leaves alternate; pinnately divided; toothless; leaflets fold together when touched. Blooms July-September in thickets, meadows, waste areas and along roadsides. Range: Ontario to Minnesota, south to the Gulf States.

Sicklepod *Cassia tora*
Small, yellow pea-like flowers resembling wild senna; long sickle-like seedpods. Leaves alternate; divided into two or three oval pairs of leaflets; toothless; stalked. Blooms July-September along stream banks and in waste areas. Range: Pennsylvania to Missouri, south to the Gulf States and the West Indies.

Yellow/Orange

Pea Family *Leguminosae*

Rattlebox *Crotalaria mucronata*

Small, bright yellow, pea-shaped flowers in a showy spike; lower petal resembles an upward, hooked spur. Leaves alternate; divided into three leaflets; ovate-oval; toothless; long stalked. Blooms June-September in fields, meadows, waste areas and along roadsides. Range: North Carolina south to Florida.

Rabbit Bells *Crotalaria spectabilis*

Large, beautiful, bright yellow pea-like flowers in a showy spike. Leaves alternate; ovate; toothless; short stalked. Blooms throughout the year in waste areas, fields, and along roadsides. Range: Virginia to Missouri, south to the Gulf States.

Pea Family   *Leguminosae*

Bagpod   *Glottidium vesicarium*
Yellow pea-like flowers in long drooping clusters from leaf axils; fruit is pea-like pods. Leaves alternate; pinnately divided 24-50 narrow, oblong leaflets; toothless. Blooms July-September in thickets, the coastal plain, and along roadsides. Range: North Carolina south to the Gulf States.

Indian Clover   *Melilotus indicus*
Tiny yellow flowers in numerous slender spikes growing out of leaf axils. Leaves alternate; divided into threes; ovate-oval; toothed; stalked. Blooms May-October in waste areas on the coastal plain. Range: The Gulf States.

Pea Family *Leguminosae*

Yellow Sweet Clover *Melilotus officinalis*
Numerous yellow flowers arranged in long, narrow clusters arising from leaf axils; have a vanilla-like odor when crushed or dried. Leaves alternate; divided into threes; toothed; stalked. Blooms May-October in fields, meadows, waste areas, and along roadsides. Range: Quebec to Ontario, south to Missouri and the Gulf States.

Decumbent Pencil-flower
Stylosanthes riparia
Orange, yellow or cream pea-like flowers. Leaves alternate; divided into threes; linear; toothless; stalkless. Blooms June-September in woods and on barren slopes. Range: New York to Missouri, south to the Gulf States.

Yellow/Orange

Bladderwort Family *Lentibulariaceae*

Horned Bladderwort
Utricularia cornuta

Yellow flower has two lips and a spur that is longer than the lower lip; scaly stalk; main portion of plant embedded in mud. Leaves alternate; linear. Blooms June-September in bogs, swamps, marshes and muddy shores of lakes. Range: Ontario to Quebec, south to Mississippi and Florida.

Swamp Bladderwort *Utricularia fibrosa*

Yellow flower with two lips and a spur about as long as lower lip. Leaves forked with hair-like segments on floating stems. Blooms May-September in marshes, swamps, bogs and along canal ditches. Range: New York and Pennsylvania south to Mississippi and Florida.

Yellow/Orange

Mallow Family *Malvaceae*

Sida *Sida rhombifolia*
Pale yellow or cream-white flowers arising from leaf axils; stalks longer than leaf stalks; often have red base. Leaves alternate; lanceolate; toothed. Blooms throughout the year in waste areas and along roadsides. Range: North Carolina to the Gulf States.

Prickly Sida *Sida spinosa*
Five-petaled, pale yellow flowers in leaf axils; stalked. Leaves opposite; arrowhead shaped; toothed; well stalked; often a spine at leaf base. Blooms June-October in waste areas and fields. Range: Massachusetts to Iowa and Missouri, south to Florida.

Yellow/Orange

Waterlily Family   *Nymphaeaceae*

American Lotus   *Nelumbo lutea*

Pale yellow flower with numerous pistils in pits on a disk-like elevated receptacle. Leaves circular; toothless; 1-2 feet wide; stem attaches to leaf at center. Blooms July-September in ponds, lakes and fast moving streams. Range: New York to Ontario, south to the Gulf States.

Yellow Pondlily   *Nuphar luteum*

Bright yellow globe-shaped blossoms; 2-3 inches across. Leaves are ovate-oval with a V-shaped notch at base; toothless. Both flowers and leaves usually float on water or sometimes slightly above water. Blooms April-October in swamps, ponds and fast moving streams. Range: Nova Scotia to Ontario, south to Louisiana and Florida.

Yellow/Orange

Waterlily Family   *Nymphaeaceae*

Cow Pea   *Vigna luteola*
Pale yellow pea-like flower; upper petal much wider than the length of the flower. Leaves alternate; divided into threes; lanceolate; toothless. A vine-like plant that climbs over surrounding plants. Blooms April-October in waste areas, woods, marshes, and along beaches and lakes. Range: The Gulf States to the West Indies.

Evening-primrose Family   *Onagraceae*

Seedbox   *Ludwigia alternifolia*
Yellow, four petaled flowers in leaf axils. Leaves alternate; lanceolate; toothless; short stalked. Blooms May-October in marshes, swamps and wet meadows. Range: Massachusetts to Iowa and Missouri, south to the Gulf States.

Evening-primrose Family   *Onagraceae*

Large Primrose Willow   *Ludwigia peruviana*
Single, large four-petaled yellow flower arising out of leaf axil; eight stamens; up to 2 inches across. Leaves alternate; oval; toothless; pointed tips; dark green; 3-6 inches long. Blooms throughout the year in ditches, canal banks, swamps, edges of ponds, and along roadsides. Range: The Gulf States.

Common Evening-primrose
Oenothera biennis
Pale yellow four-petaled flower with long, slender calyx tube; stem is erect, stout and hairy. Leaves alternate; lanceolate; toothed; stalkless. Blooms June-September in meadows, fields and along roadsides. Range: Quebec to Ontario and Minnesota, south to the Gulf States.

Yellow/Orange

Evening-primrose Family   *Onagraceae*

Cut-leaf Evening-primrose   *Oenothera laciniata*
Pale yellow four-petaled flowers in leaf axils; up to 2 inches across; tip of each petal is notched. Leaves alternate; oak-like; deeply toothed or lobed; short stalked; 1-3 inches long. Blooms March-October in fields, waste areas and along roadsides. Range: New Jersey to Minnesota, south to the Gulf States.

Wood-sorrel Family   *Oxalidaceae*

Upright Yellow Wood-sorrel   *Oxalis stricta*
Yellow five-petaled flowers, often marked with red at the base; flowers not on separate stalks. Leaves alternate; long stalked; three leaflets; tips notched; toothless. Blooms May-October in woods, fields, meadows and along roadsides. Range: Quebec to Minnesota, south to the Gulf States.

Milkwort Family *Polygalaceae*

Yellow Milkwort *Polygala lutea*
Bright orange-yellow, globe-shaped flowers; only milkwort with blossoms this color. Leaves alternate; narrow-ovate; toothless; stalkless; numerous. Blooms April-October in coastal plain bogs and pinelands. Range: New York south to Louisiana and Florida.

Low Pine-barren Milkwort *Polygala ramrosa*
Sulfur-yellow flowers in dense, flat-topped clusters. Upper leaves alternate; small; narrow. Basal leaves rosette; ovate-lanceolate; toothless. Blooms June-September in wet coastal plain pinelands. Range: New Jersey, south to the Gulf States.

Yellow/Orange   115

Milkwort Family *Polygalaceae*

Yellow Bachelor's Button *Polygala rugelii*
Dense lemon yellow globe-shaped cluster of flowers at the tip of a single stem. Leaves alternate; lanceolate; toothless. Blooms May-September in swamps, moist areas and low pinelands. Range: Florida.

Primrose Family *Primulaceae*

Fringed Loosestrife *Lysimachia ciliata*
Yellow five-petaled flowers with fringed margins; a tiny point at the tip. Leaves opposite; narrowly ovate; toothless; stalked; fringed hairs on leaf stalks. Blooms June-September in swamps, wet places and along roadsides. Range: Quebec to Ontario and Minnesota, south to the Gulf States.

Snapdragon Family *Scrophulariaceae*

Smooth False Foxglove
Gerardia laevigata

Yellow, roundish, five-lobed, trumpet-like flowers in leaf axils; 1-2 inches across. Leaves opposite; lanceolate; pinnately cleft; 4-6 inches long, upper leaves smaller; toothed or toothless; narrow. Blooms July-September in dry or moist woods and along roadsides. Range: Pennsylvania to Ohio, south to Tennessee and Florida.

Butter And Eggs *Linaria vulgaris*

Bright yellow flowers having a prominent orange palate on the lower lip; long, slender curved spur; showy spikes. Leaves alternate; linear; toothless; short stalked. Blooms May-October in fields, meadows, waste areas and along roadsides. Range: Quebec to Ontario and Minnesota, south to the Gulf States.

Yellow/Orange

Snapdragon Family *Scrophulariaceae*

Cassia Seymeria
Seymeria cassioides
Bright yellow tubular flower with six, unequal flaring lobes; pale yellow corolla; flowers scattered along stem. Leaves alternate; pinnately cleft; narrow slender segments. Blooms June-October in dry pinelands and hammocks on the coastal plain. Range: North Carolina to Louisiana and Florida.

Seymeria *Seymeria pectinata*
Bright yellow tubular flower with five unequal, flaring petal-like lobes; deep yellow corolla; spotted with red. Leaves alternate; pinnately cleft; lobes of leaves lanceolate. Blooms September-October in sandy pinelands on the coastal plain. Range: South Carolina to Louisiana and Florida.

Yellow/Orange

Snapdragon Family   *Scrophulariaceae*

Common Mullein
Verbascum thapsus

Five-petaled yellow flowers at the tip of a wand-like leafy stem. Leaves alternate on stem, rosette at base; toothless; stalkless to flowing onto stem; grayish-green; flannel-like; soft; stem rigid. Blooms June-September in fields, meadows, waste areas and along roadsides. Range: Nova Scotia to Quebec and Ontario, south to the Gulf States.

Vervain Family   *Verbenaceae*

Shrub Verbena   *Lantana camara*

Tiny white, yellow, pink or orange five-petaled flowers in roundish clusters at ends of long stalks. Leaves opposite; ovate-heart shaped; toothed; stalked. Blooms May-November in waste areas. Range: Florida to the West Indies.

Yellow-eyed Grass Family *Xyridaceae*

Yellow-eyed Grass *Xyris flexuosa*

Small yellow three-petaled flower on a scaly, cone-like head. Leaves are very long, slender and grass-like; wiry, slender flower stalk is separate and longer than leaf stalks. Blooms June-September on the coastal plain. Range: Maine to Wisconsin, south to Missouri and the Gulf States.

Caltrop Family *Zygophyllaceae*

Tribulus *Tribulus cistoides*

Bright yellow, five-petaled flower with ten stamens and one pistil; five sepals. Leaves opposite; divided pinnately into paired segments. Blooms March-September in hammocks, waste areas, and along roadsides. Range: The Gulf States.

Yellow/Orange

Index

Index

Index